THIS
PROVERB

A PLAY BY
BEN TOMOLOJU

Copyright © 2020 Ben Tomoloju

ISBN:
978-1-952874-23-9 (paperback)
978-1-952874-24-6 (hardback)
978-1-952874-25-3 (ebook)

All rights reserved. No part of this publication may be reproduced, stored in a retrieval system, or transmitted in any form or by any means - electronic, mechanical, photocopy, recording, scanning, or other – except for brief quotations in critical reviews or articles, without the prior written permission of the author and the publisher.

Printed in New York by:

OMNIBOOK CO.
99 Wall Street, Suite 118
New York, NY 10005
USA
+1-866-216-9965
www.omnibookcompany.com

First Edition

For e-book purchase: Kindle on Amazon, Barnes and Noble
Book purchase: Amazon.com, Barnes & Noble, and
www.omnibookcompany.com

Omnibook titles may be purchased in bulk for educational, business, fund-raising, or sales promotional use. For more information please e-mail info@omnibookcompany.com

Cover illustration by Akeem Anishere
This publication is sponsored by Kola Olawoyin, Kayode Tomoloju, Jahman Anikulapo, Akeem Anishere and Sunday Adewale.

CONTENTS

AUTHOR'S NOTE — 1
CHARACTERS — 2

ACT ONE

FIRST MOVEMENT — 3
SECOND MOVEMENT — 13
THIRD MOVEMENT — 17
FOURTH MOVEMENT — 27

ACT TWO

FIRST MOVEMENT — 29
SECOND MOVEMENT — 43
THIRD MOVEMENT — 63
FOURTH MOVEMENT — 79

ACT THREE

FIRST MOVEMENT — 85
SECOND MOVEMENT — 93
THIRD MOVEMENT — 99

CONCLUSION — 103

AUTHOR'S NOTE

In 1974, at the age of nineteen, and as a student of Christ's School, Ado-Ekiti, in the old Western State of Nigeria, I reflected on the inter-generational crises that had placed the African youth at a disadvantaged position in the general scheme of things. I wrote a play titled *THE WALNUT* in long hand for performance by my high school drama society as a student of the now globally renowned poet and scholar-critic, Distinguished Professor Niyi Osundare. Unfortunately, the production was aborted and the script lost, but the story remained intact in one's imagination. Due to the nagging pressure of the theme and its currency in the socio-political equation of my country, the story had to be revisited.

In 1981, just a couple of years into Nigeria's Second Republic, one was astonished that politicians had learnt nothing after thirteen years of military interregnum (1966-1979). Bitter rivalry culminating in insidious schemes were the order of the day. Rapacious appetite for ill-gotten wealth and socially debilitating peddling of influences were so pervasive that the social contract was massively affronted. Again, the young breed was at the losing end. Jobs were scarce. Confidence waned. Crime rate escalated. Politicians pursued their selfish agenda, least concerned with the rights of posterity.

THE WALNUT was re-written under a new title, *THIS PROVERB*, in 1981, as a re-affirmation of one's concern for the well-being of the members of this generation constantly referred to as the leaders of tomorrow. The pusillanimity of current leaders in the face of truth, their predilection for mischief and moral bankruptcy obliterates visions and ideas canvassed for the upliftment of society. Instead of positive transformation, society harvests anarchy. Tragedy not only looms across time and space but is sometimes let loose consuming even the innocent. This is the burden that has continued to plague the populace one generation after another.

CHARACTERS

Adeboye	–	The Hermit
Alaye	–	King of Jokoje
Adewale	–	Son of Adeboye / Regent
Morola	–	Adeboye's wife
Maadan	–	Alaye's youngest wife
Elegbara	–	Divinity of the Crossroads
Ifagbaye	–	Chief Priest

Balogun
Dakeja
Ojomo   – High Chiefs of Jokoje
Sapatira

Mogaji	–	Junior Chief
Baiko	–	Son of Dakeja
Jibola	–	Son of Balogun
Okitikata	–	Palace factotum / Law enforcer

Praise Singer
Leader
Woman
Man One
Man Two

Spirits, Singers, Drummers, People

ACT ONE : FIRST MOVEMENT

(Alaye's Palace. Morning. Lighting is bleary, barely showing some ritual objects – mainly objects of worship – strategically placed at various corners of the palace reception where they do not impede the movements of guests. From both wings, women arrayed in ritual costumes file in, singing homiletic songs to herald the entry of the King, their dance accentuating the act of paying homage.)

Ojo ro sibee o eee
Let the rain fall right here
Orun ran je'mi r'ubo me ire
The sun, shine that I may see my route
Ero ya, j'emi lo
Folks, give way and let me go
Ero ya jare ma ba 'on de be
Give way that I may join them
Ma yun'le oloye mi
To my Chieftain's home

LEAD:
Ko s'owo owuro
Even in the morning

CHORUS:
Ma yun'le oloye mi
I'll go to my Chieftain's home

LEAD:
Ko ba se ni osan gangan
Be it at high noon

CHORUS:
Ma yun'le oloye mi
I'll go to my Chieftain's home

LEAD:
Ko ba se l'oganjo oru
If it is in the dead of night

CHORUS:
Ma yun'le oloye mi
I'll go to my Chieftain's home

(The voice of the Palace Poet is raised over the refrain as he steps into the scene gracefully, chanting the King's praise-chant.)

SINGER:
Mo ki o loni o
I salute you
Omo a f'okun s'onarin
Whose walkway is the sea
Omo abinalenu bi aro aya apeja
Mouth flaring like hearth of a fisher's wife
Olori oko, eleru l'ona
Jungle-master, owner of road treasures
Erujeje l'oju omo ar'aye
Fear in the eyes of humans
Kaabiyesi ooo
Kaabiyesi ooo

(An ensemble of talking-drummers charge the scene with explosive syncopation detailed on the special praise-chant heralding the King's approach - 'Eru Oba ni mo ba, Oba to.' The drummers weave dance-steps to complement those of the women. In the middle of the singing, dancing and drumming, Oba Alaye enters magnificently in his royal robe. The King stands still, absorbing with rapt attention, the display by his subjects. He adjusts the expansive sleeve of his over-garment. The performance stops abruptly. His subjects kneel or prostrate in obeisance as tradition demands of their gender respectively. Alaye's visage is awash with a bright smile. He waves his horsetail in a bold gesture at his subjects who take their cues and depart through the wings, singing:

This Proverb

    Arobafin l'Oba npa
        Whoever insults the King, he kills
    Arobafin l'Oba npa
        Whoever insults the King, he kills
    Alaye gba mi s'ile l'owo arobafin
        Alaye deliver me from the insolent one
    Arobafin l'Oba npa...
        Whoever insults the King, he kills...

(Alaye observes them fondly as they take their exit, a bright smile on his lips.)

        ALAYE:
How I wish, once again,
To be a simple-minded folk.
(He moves to a statue right of the throne. Kneels.)
Orunmila, your wisdom is my desire now
Let it come, Olugbirin - Aringbirin;
Orunmila who treads with hefty thuds
Into the market place; I will worship you.
(Rises.)
(He moves over to another, further right.)
Obatala, Ogege, the tree that is climbed and descended with ease;
One who gives out a bride has had all favours done;
Deflect me this time from bouts of wine.
(Moves to the immediate left of the throne.)
Ogun, the daring belligerent, fierce phantom spirit
Who owns the crooked house on the way to heaven,
Spare your axe, I plead, spare your axe.
(Further left.)
And if I may turn to you, Sango, husband of Oya.
Ha! With mouth ever so wide, ever so flaming.
Scorch-tongue, the world is not yet set
To be set ablaze.

(Enter Sapatira. He waits, UPSTAGE-LEFT, watching as Alaye moves DOWN-CENTRE.)

And for every offering let us not forget Esu,
Lord of the crossroads, who goes in motley dress,
The one who walks and wings and swims
All at once. Esu! Where-are-you
And the world goes turning...

(He counts a few dance-steps before he sees Sapatira.)

Howuh! Sapatira?

SAPATIRA:
Kaabiyesi.

ALAYE:
May you live.

SAPATIRA:
Ase. **(Sits on the floor.)**

ALAYE:
I expect Ojomo and Dakeja to be here by now.

SAPATIRA:
They must be on the way.

ALAYE:
And Balogun, too.

(Enter Balogun.)

BALOGUN:
Here I am, Kabiyesi.
I am my father's son to the very name I bear. Kaabiyesii.

ALAYE:
Gbere.

(Two voices are heard singing outside.)

This Proverb

I hear voices blessing the morning with
enchanting song.
Whose may they be, I ask?

(Balogun goes to peep.)

    BALOGUN:
Dakeja and Ojomo
They are almost at the door.

(Dakeja and Ojomo enter with their song.)

Jigini-Jigini n'ile Awo
   Rich is the home of the initiate
Jigini-jigini n'ile Awo
   Rich is the home of the initiate
Okun fofo oju'le ikan
   It is loaded like the termite-hill
Ohun Oju ri o l'onka
   Loaded with countless manifests
Jigini-Jigini n'ile Awo
   Rich is the home of the initiate

    DAKEJA:
Kabiyesi o. (Sits.)

    OJOMO:
Kabiyesi. (Sits.)

    ALAYE:
Gbere o. Hmh! **(Adjusts himself on the throne.)**
He who holds live-coal in his hand
Never waits for a chat.
Let us waste no time, therefore, my trusted chiefs,
As the yam is still hot in the mouth.
Before Ifagbaye joins us to reveal
The word of Orunmila, I wish to tell
That last night, my father talked to me in a dream.

CHIEFS:
Ehe!

ALAYE:
He did talk, reminding me
Of the sacred grove that has,
For the past three years, been left
Without a Hermit.

DAKEJA:
True.

ALAYE:
You all know what that means.

SAPATIRA:
If care is not taken,
The gods' wrath may fall on Jokoje.

OJOMO:
Plague, there may be plague.

DAKEJA:
And they may hold the rain for years.

ALAYE:
And leave us and our children famished
In the famine that may befall us.
But the news of war that is announced before it comes
Never kills the cripple. We have been warned.
Hence I have invited you to this communion.
It is our fathers who say
That it is other people's wisdom
That prevents an elder from being called a fool.

CHIEFS:
Beeni.

ALAYE:
We must put our heads together.

This Proverb

(The song of Orunmila wafts in from outside into the heart of the ante-room, escorting Ifagbaye, the priest-divine, into the palace.)

Ifa jigini-jigin o o
 Ifa, the bounteous one
Ifa mo gboro kan
 Ifa, I received some news
Ifa jigini-jigin o o
 Ifa, the bounteous one
Ifa mo gboro kan
 Ifa, I received some news
Ifa gb'aye tan o
 Ifa takes over the earth
Opele m'aye gun
 The diviner's string balances the earth
Ifa gb'aye tan o
 Ifa takes over the earth
Opele m'aye gun
 The diviner's string balances the earth

Ifagbaye is here.

(The song goes on for a few more rounds. Ifagbaye enters, an old man in his ending days, stepping gracefully, his figure bent and resting on the walking- stick, his bag hanging from his shoulder. With difficulty, he sits, right in front of Alaye.)

Ifagbaye, wealth of wisdom,
The only eye in a gloomy forest.
Jokoje calls you once again,
The suppliant children of Orunmila;
They call you once again...

IFAGBAYE:
Enough, my King.
I pay my respect as due to the throne of your fathers
Which you now occupy, and majestically, too.
But I must keep sounding it in your ears
That you stop telling me what I have been told.

CHIEFS:
Unh! **(They nod their heads in the affirmative.)**

ALAYE:
Ifagbaye, your wisdom holds the world's crooked corners.
It held them for my father. Let it hold for me.

IFAGBAYE:
It will hold for you, Oba Alaye. So briefly.
But, did they not tell me that it will be over my last breath?
Age has come in its ripest, fellows,
And I am being drawn in a tug-of-war
Between the living and the dead. Impotent priest;
That is what I am, and there the pity lies.
I have no son to practice the lore
When I am gone. And go I must,
Very soon.

BALOGUN:
But what is this you are saying, Ifagbaye?

OJOMO:
Sounds like a riddle.

DAKEJA:
Is this part of the message?

IFAGBAYE:
It is ... **(Pauses. Shakes his head.)**
This is my last duty to Jokoje,
Because the tomorrow is no distant one
That will take my breath away.
This is my last duty to Jokoje,
And I must perform it with perfection
As always I have done.
Listen.

CHIEFS:
Unh! **(Impatiently, they scratch and shift hither and thither.)**

This Proverb

IFAGBAYE:
(Casts his divination string.) Alaye.

ALAYE:
I'm listening.

IFAGBAYE:
They tell me to tell you
That there is no need to worry.
A spectacle suddenly met
Differs much from one foreboded.
They have found you the Hermit!

CHIEFS:
Ahah!

ALAYE:
That is one problem solved.
Who is he?

IFAGBAYE:
He is a father of Jokoje,
One who should sit on the throne after you.
He lives in the city.

BALOGUN:
That must be Adeboye.

DAKEJA:
Adeboye ke?

IFAGBAYE:
That is the Hermit,
The second in rank to Alaye.
I am sent, fellows,
I do not send myself.
The order rests with those who send me.
And they tell me to warn,
That the damask of wisdom which in me
Shall seem a shroud
Shall live again with the son of Adeboye
When I am gone,

If and only if the rabbit
Does not betray the trust of Ifa.
So I am done, and I must go. **(Starts packing.)**

ALAYE:
Father of wisdom, blessings.
Your service is invaluable to this clan.
All you have said we shall keep
In the left hand, that we may not feed
With it and lose it.
And to you, my chiefs, the job,
You should know, is at hand.
Dakeja, Ojomo and Sapatira.

THE THREE:
Kabiyesi.

ALAYE:
Tomorrow, you shall set out for the city.
Go and tell Adeboye to make preparations to come home.
You will tell him this:
The gods and the people of Jokoje
Desire his service as the Hermit of the Sacred Grove
Until I go to the world where the elders go
And he takes over the throne.
Ifagbaye, is that a wise message?

IFAGBAYE:
It is wise. **(On his feet.)**
They are the words of the gods.
Their deeds are rightly done.
Let no man misconstrue the message.
And if anyone wrongs the right,
Ifagbaye may be no more
To heed to any call.
My feet are on their way home, Kabiyesi.
I must follow them.

(Goes out with the song 'Ifa Jigini-jigin' while the rest stare at him until the lights fade out.)

ACT ONE : SECOND MOVEMENT

(At a distance off-stage-left, nearer gangway-right, Ojomo, Dakeja and Sapatira are heard first, seen later, trekking wearily and in dialogue.)

SAPATIRA:
Is it still far away?

OJOMO:
Not too far, Sapatira, but
The weariness makes it seem so.
My old bones, my old bones are almost cracking,
Sapatira.
It seems I am going to faint.
I need a rest.

SAPATIRA:
And who doesn't need a rest?
We all do. But there is an urgent message
Handed down for us to deliver
By our Lord and King, Alaye.

OJOMO:
An urgent message for the city-dweller,
And so I, Ojomo, should break my bones?
You talk like a baby, babble like an infant
With oiled lips. Must I die before my time,
Bearing a message to the city-dweller?

SAPATIRA:
And why, Ojomo?
Why did you not say this before Alaye?

OJOMO:
But Alaye should know
That it's unbecoming
For a whole chief to be treated
Like a court-messenger, shouldn't he?
Did our fathers not say that
Wherever you call your head

Is never used to step on the ground?
Hen, Dakeja!

DAKEJA:
Look, I am hungry.
Hunger cares not if there is no cowrie in the house.
Every sunrise tells of the rise of hunger.
I am hungry.

SAPATIRA:
Let us go on.
Adeboye's house lies
At the outskirt of the city.
We shall soon get there.

(They wobble towards a tree off-stage left.)

Besides ...

(Before he could go on Ojomo has fallen.)

DAKEJA:
(Surprised.) What!

SAPATIRA:
Ojomo!

OJOMO:
Ugh! Ugh!! Ugh!!!...

DAKEJA:
Too weary to stand. Ojomo!
Let us bear him to yonder tree
And feed him with fried plantain.

(They carry Ojomo to the tree, massage his muscles.)

This is what I say:
Are there no better heads in Jokoje
To be the Hermit of the sacred grove
That a man must languish on the road

This Proverb

In a bid to catch a city frog?

SAPATIRA:
I have news to tell when I get home.
It is the traveller that tells the news of Abiona.
I have news to tell when I get home.

OJOMO:
(Regaining consciousness. Faint voice.)
A little water to wet my parchy throat.

SAPATIRA:
(Searches his bag for the water-jar. Brings it out.)
Here. And a little water
To wash your withering face.

DAKEJA:
And the fried plantain;
(Brings out a wrap of fried plantain from his bag.)
Here, let us eat.

(Ojomo rises to sit with the rest on the ground. They eat in silence. They finish eating. Dakeja returns the rest of the food into his bag.)

OJOMO:
(Rises.)
Are we set to go? **(Others rise.)**

DAKEJA:
To the house of Adeboye.

SAPATIRA:
Yes.

ALL:
Let us proceed, therefore, with the pain,
With the pain of making a man
Whose dawn is our sinister night.

Let us proceed to the house of Adeboye.

(They start crossing to down stage-right...)

It is not like going to win a bride, dear friends;
I mean this trip.
And that is what grips us within.
But let us proceed, let us proceed
Watching ourselves withering along the road.

(A song is raised by Dakeja. They wobble to its rhythm, singing in unison.)

    DAKEJA:
Eyi mo ya
   This is my destiny
Eyi mo ya re
   This one is my destiny
Eyikun ti b'aye lo
   The rest has disappeared with the world

    CHORUS:
One n'agbara
   The powerful one
One n'agbara ju'ne
   Who is more powerful than you
Re mi d'owo one mu
   Is the one
Figba n'erun
   Who can slap you with your own hand
Oran aye le
   The affair of this world is hectic
Eru aye papoju o kookoo.
   The burden of this world is overwhelming

ACT ONE : THIRD MOVEMENT

(The chiefs have arrived at Adeboye's house. They are seated in the parlour, a cosy room situated at the top-level rectangular platform centre-stage, set before the lights come on. They make a poetic rendition of their roles. Adeboye is seated in the middle, a white wrapper thrown over his shoulder, watching meditatively. They all sit over bowls of wine.)

CHIEFS:
We are the elders of Jokoje.
We are the servants and slaves of Jokoje.
We are sent by our lord and master
To deliver a message to the city-dweller.

DAKEJA:
Here is the city-dweller
On whose account I trekked here with bile.

OJOMO:
Here is the city-dweller
On whose account I swooned on my way here.

SAPATIRA:
Here is the city-dweller
On whose account I wear a dusty cap.

ADEBOYE:
Give your message!

DAKEJA:
Through what course will the message flow,
But the river of bitterness which brought us here?
You sit here asking for a message
Like a new bride for most resplendent jewel.
She should know
That it costs money and sweat to buy the jewel.
He who passes stool does not feel the smell,
It is the one who packs it that feels the smell.

We are the nightsoilmen of Jokoje.
And we do not blame your airs,
We do not blame the manner of your books,
To sit on the arm-chair
And ask for the message.

OJOMO:
The manner of your books,
The manner of your education.

CHIEFS:
We do not blame the manner of your civilization,
To sit on the arm-chair
And ask for the message.

(Enter Morola.)

MOROLA:
My chiefs and fathers, **(Kneels.)**
The pillars in the four corners
Of my chamber of love,
Shall I bring your food?

SAPATIRA:
(Snappily.) No food!

MOROLA:
Enh? **(Embarrassed)**

DAKEJA:
Our dear wife, Morola,
The matter at hand is too demanding
To allow a feel of hunger.
When we are through, you will know where we stand.

ADEBOYE:
Morola, my wife,
When they are through you will know where I stand.
For now you may dismiss yourself.
Call me Adewale to come and greet the chiefs.

This Proverb

MOROLA:
Oooo. **(Exit.)** Adewale-e-e... **(Within.)**

ADEWALE:
(Within.) Yes Mummy.

ADEBOYE:
Now, elders of Jokoje,
You have come as you were sent,
But you have not done what you were sent to do.
Is it not known that one should not neglect
The treatment of leprosy
And begin to treat ringworm?
I presume that the wine before us
Is potent enough to force out even the news of death.
Why then do you go on
Stretching my eagerness with your rigmarole?

OJOMO:
Hear him;
He calls us rigmarole.

SAPATIRA:
Whether a rig maroles
Or it does not marole,
A rig is a rig.
We are sober servants of our land.
Our role is defined within us,
And it is beyond the rigmarole of your education.
There is only one side to it, not two.
There is only one side, too, to the message we bring.
If you will...

ADEBOYE:
Look, I'm beginning to lose my temper.
Must you continue to torture my mind
With your vacillation?
Alaye has sent you with a message to me.
Then say it, or go back to Jokoje
And sleep with your concubines.

CHIEFS:
That to us?

ADEBOYE:
Go back with no trophies on your heads
If you fail to bear well what is placed in your hands.
(Pause. Everyone is tense.)
I mean, I am the heir-apparent
To the throne of Jokoje.
I have the right to know the state of things
In the home of my birth,
In the land which my fathers nurtured.
Alaye acts well by treating me to my right.
But here you are, mingy middlemen,
Who seek to stifle the generation of goodwill
Between one party and another.

DAKEJA:
The dove pronounces his incantations
And thinks that the pigeon does not understand.
The pigeon understands.

CHIEFS:
He is only pretending not to notice it.

DAKEJA:
Adeboye, the son of Ade-Oloko,
We know your worth in Jokoje.
We know it as much as we know our worthlessness.
But let us leave our own worthlessness aside.
It is on account of your worth that we have come.
It is on account of your worth
That Ifa-Agboniregun selects you
To take over as the Hermit of the sacred grove.

ADEBOYE:
Hermit!

SAPATIRA:
It does not go beyond that.
The King has been warned in a dream.

This Proverb

Ifagbaye, the servant of Orunmila,
Has mentioned Adeboye, the city-dweller.
We have been sent.
We do not send ourselves.
The order rests with those who send us.
It does not go beyond that.

ADEBOYE:
And is there no other explanation?
No other...

OJOMO:
You never lick hot soup in a hurry.
There is no explanation beyond the act.
Prepare yourself and come home...

(Enter Adewale.)

Ah! Is this the baby I used to know?

ADEBOYE:
Eh, that is Adewale, my first child.
He is almost a man now.

DAKEJA:
Enough to swallow his father.
Come this way son, and take my blessing.

(Adewale prostrates.)

May you grow old.

ALL:
Ase.

SAPATIRA:
Adewale, omo Ogbontarigi Umale;
The one who drove the iroko spirits out
And usurped their tree for his home,
Omo Anjonu-Iberu, Ade-Oloko,
Whose breath causes tremor
In the grove of Elegbara,

The very image of Adeboye,
Gbere, my son.

    ADEWALE:
Thank you, chief.

    DAKEJA:
Take this fried plantain, my son,
And share it with your younger ones.

    ADEWALE:
Thanks you, chief.

    DAKEJA:
You may go.

(Exit Adewale. Dakeja sighs a big one and is soon on his feet.)

Adeboye, our mission is ended.

    ADEBOYE:
Good friends, my gratitude is unreserved.
Elders of Jokoje, I pay my respect as due.
The message you have brought is
At once distracting,
At once gratifying.
In my speechless moments
Before you came out with the news,
I had thought and seen myself
In demand for something urgent.
And my premeditation has killed surprise.
It has bought for me, courage as a cheap adze
To fell the reign of perplexity.
I am a man whose mind is made up.
I shall be the king someday.
And since I do not wish for disorder when I am king,
I should not be the cause of disorder
During another king's reign.
Therefore, tell Alaye that I will not disappoint him.

This Proverb

Tell Jokoje that I will not disappoint her.
I will come home as soon
As I have equipped my family
With enough to last them for my period of sequestration.

DAKEJA:
You have spoken well.
And now that you have agreed without reservation
To heed the call of your people,
We poor slaves may saunter back home
With the blessed smile your acquiescence has brought.
Where is the mother of the house?

ADEBOYE:
Morola-a-a . .

MOROLA:
Oooo! **(Appears.)** Here I am.

ADEBOYE:
The chiefs are set to go. **(Soon falls into a reverie. The chiefs rise.)**

MOROLA:
Go to where?
You shall not waste my pounded yam, chiefs.
I did not marry your son to have my cooking rebuffed.
If you are so much in a hurry to go,
I shall put the food in your bags
For you to eat on your way.

SAPATIRA:
Good wife, bring it. **(Exit Morola.)**
It is a wife who cares for her husband
That clears the booty of the husband.

(Re-enter Morola.)

MOROLA:
Here. **(She puts the food into Dakeja's bag.)**
That should keep your stomachs turgid
For the stretch of your journey.

OJOMO:
Thanks you, woman.
May you continue to be the glitter in our eyes.

MOROLA:
Ase. **(Freezes on a spot to a special lighting effect depicting a generally confounding mood.)**

CHIEFS:
We have come long.
We shall go long.
It is a long and tedious travel.
We would have wished it otherwise.
But what use is a wish in the stomach of a python?
There is no will in us,
But the bile of subservience. **(They break from the frozen posture, moving out slowly.)**

DAKEJA:
Ah least we have done what we were sent to do.

OJOMO:
We have grudgingly done what we were sent here to do.

SAPATIRA:
Let the slave return from bondage to bondage.

DAKEJA:
But let him be consoled; there is no difference
Between birth and birth.

OJOMO:
The birth of a slave
Is like the birth of a freeborn.

This Proverb

SAPATIRA:
And the slave deserves a little thank, at least.

DAKEJA:
Yes, Opeloyeru. Let us go.
The slave deserves a little thank.
Let us go and chase another word of thanks.

(He raises the old song again.)

DAKEJA:
Eyi mo ya
  This is my destiny
Eyi mo ya re
  This is my destiny
Eyikun ti b'aye lo
  The rest has gone with the world

CHORUS:
One n'agbara
  The powerful one
One n'agbara ju'ne
  Who is more powerful than you
Re mi d'owo one mu
  Is the one
Figba n'erun
  Who can slap you with your own hand
Oran aye le
  The affair of this world is hectic
Eru aye papoju o ko koo .
  The burden of this world is overwhelming

(While the chiefs are taking a gradual exit, Morola rushes to her husband. She taps him ceaselessly to express her confusion over the chiefs' mystified bearing. Adeboye is shocked out of his reverie. He rises, Morola in his arms. . . He calls as the song runs to an end.)

ADEBOYE:
Halt! Elders of Jokoje...
Halt! One more question. **(Song stops.)**
They are gone.

(Adewale and Teniola rush in. They halt at strategic positions. All eyes on their parents.)

It was like a dream the way they came.
Still, the way they left was like a dream.
Then I saw an active stem in a dream,
Struggling and struggling...**(Goes back to sit.)**
My wife, Morola, **(She sits by his side.)**
My son, Adewale, **(He kneels by his right.)**
My daughter, Teniola, **(She kneels by his left.)**
Come.
There is something I want to tell you...

(Lights fade off gradually – in this position – backed by the trilling of percussions.)

ACT ONE : FOURTH MOVEMENT

(Spotlight on Adeboye, now in a danshiki and trousers, occasionally miming to his speech.)

        ADEBOYE:
Alone I wing my way towards Jokoje,
Leaving behind the love I know, the love I make,
Towards the mystery I do not know.
Alone I wing toward the height of it
Like the eagle.
I wash myself towards the whiteness of the dove,
Leaving behind the blood akin to mine,
Approaching the heart of the mystery of purity.
Let me go, let me go and be a Hermit,
Sequestered from known affection, unknown hate.
There is the road. Rise,
Son of the soil, rise
And prove allegiance right in any sense.
There is the road,
Take your dream along with your feet.
The soil of Jokoje waits warmly
To be marked by your footfalls ...
As if I were a different person.
And if I am two different persons
Let me listen to me this time;
A grave communion in my duality.
I owe a duty to my land
And to the people of my land,
The performance of which
Is a desire exigent... I owe all!
I owe, I swim towards the repayment of what I owe.
Alone I swim my way towards Jokoje,
Leaving behind the love I know, the love I make,
Towards the mystery I do not know.
A Hermit; what is it not to be a Hermit,
Not to feel the freshness of a spirit,
Not to be the link for animist souls –
What is it not to be the heart of the matter?
Dismiss me.

I am a man whose mind is made up.
If... there is no if.
Conditions are for novices...
Dakeja, Ojomo and Sapatira,
Tell Alaye I will not... You may go.
I will follow.
Tell the people to prepare for my installation;
The Hermit... Yes, you may go.
I will follow.
And here I am.
Alone I dance my way towards Jokoje,
Leaving behind the love I know, the love I make.
Alone I dance my way
Towards the mystery I do not know.

(Lights fade off.)

ACT TWO : FIRST MOVEMENT

(Alaye's palace. Balogun, Dakeja, Ojomo and Sapatira are seated, awaiting the arrival of Alaye, dressed to match the occasion. The village pageant will soon be around. Meanwhile they engage in discussions.)

    BALOGUN:
Perhaps I did not hear you well, Ojomo.
Did you say the new Hermit slighted you
When you visited him in the city?

    DAKEJA:
Perhaps I do not know again
What it is to be insulted.
I would not blame him.
It was his master who made us mats,
So he found it easy to tread on us.
Had it not been for common breeding,
What will bring a pigeon into the midst of chickens?

    BALOGUN:
Caution, Dakeja,
I saw jaundice in your eyes as you spoke.
What has Adeboye done
To deserve such hatred ?...

    SAPATIRA:
Do not go amiss, Balogun.
I seal your mouth with money and children.
Let me talk. It is no jaundice.
We bear no malice against the city-dweller.

    BALOGUN:
Insidious schemers! Who does not know your plans?
One by one you break your own ladders,
Ending up as scrap or litter.
One by one you head for the hill of wastes.
Vanity beclouds your hollowness
And empty men are spared to live.

OJOMO:
Infidel! Do you have no sympathy
For the sons of the gods?

BALOGUN:
What god would sanction
Your dark scheme against a man
Of such unparalleled nobility?
Leave the gods out of this, Ojomo,
And find another reason.

SAPATIRA:
And leave yourself out of this, Balogun,
If you know you are so bereft of reason.

BALOGUN:
You said that to me, Sapatira?
(Gets up, advances towards Sapatira.)

SAPATIRA:
I said it to you, Balogun.
(Stands at alert.)

BALOGUN:
You... **(Pushes Sapatira who lands on his buttock, advances, but Dakeja intervenes.)**

OJOMO:
Eewoh!

DAKEJA:
This shall never happen in my presence.
Balogun, stay away.
How shall it be heard
That the mighty tree whose canopy
Protects the forest
Has now come to bow so low?

BALOGUN:
Why didn't you let me teach him
A thing or two?
Then he would know

This Proverb

That even if the tiger forfeits his dinner
He is still more than a match for the dog.

SAPATIRA:
You're only bragging.
Too much mouth and no action

BALOGUN:
You heard that again? **(Advances, restrained.)**

OJOMO:
No, don't.

BALOGUN:
Alright. Let me go and urinate and come back.
Then you will know
That I am Balogun,
The son of Ekun Okeho.
Let me go and urinate and come back.
(Exit. Loosening his trousers.)

SAPATIRA:
(Makes a belated attempt to fight back.)
Why didn't he come again?
I was waiting to give him
One last bit of bitterness.
He thought he could push me
And get my back on the ground.
He needs to know, anyway,
That the back of a cat never touches the gound.

OJOMO:
Enough. You, sit down.
One never gets so angry with the head
As to wear his hat on his buttocks.
Let us walk our feet on a place
Where there is a path.

SAPATIRA:
Ko buru... Imagine!
He wants to defend Adeboye.
Adeboye is a thief;

Let us say it frankly.
He has only come from the city
To steal the medal
Which we spent our lifetime
To win. Just overnight,
And he is everybody's hero
While we are everybody's fools.
We ask for something to love,
A beautiful thing comes out
What happens if it is beautiful and is not loved?

DAKEJA:
There it must be resolved.
And if our fathers said
That the kolanut ripens in an elder's mouth,
He does not have to chew the pads of his jaw
With it.

OJOMO:
That is true.

DAKEJA:
We have discovered that Alaye
Will not be using his royal staff today
For the royal procession.
Rather, he will bear the white calabash
For the offering at the sacred grove.
What then stops us
From laying our hands
On the King's royal staff
And bring the thieving upon Adeboye?

OJOMO:
Hmn! How shall we...

DAKEJA:
No hesitation, Ojomo.
This is a matter of do or don't.
If you shall bear OSHAKA,
Let us call you OSHAKA.
If you shall bear OSHOKO,
Let us call you OSHOKO.

This Proverb

But we refuse to recognise OSHAKANSHOKO,
The name of the fickling feather
Which moves with the winds without a will.
Let me know now, Ojomo,
If you are with me or not.

    OJOMO:
I am with you.

    SAPATIRA:
And I will take the royal staff,
Steal the royal staff and plant the fault on the
Worthless city-dweller.

    DAKEJA:
You will take it from the King's inner-chamber?

    SAPATIRA:
So long as my name is Sapatira.

    DAKEJA:
That is solved.

(The voice of a royal bard is heard from within.)

    ROYAL BARD:
Mo ki o l'oni oooooo
   I salute you
Omo a fo'kun s'ona rin.
   Whose walkway is the sea
Omo ab'ina l'enu bi aro aya apeja.
   Mouth flaring like hearth of a fisher's wife
Olori oko, eleru l'ona,
   Jungle-master, owner of road-treasures
Eru jeje l'oju omo araye,
   Fear in the eyes of humans
Kaaabiyesi oooooo!

    DAKEJA:
I can hear the king's bard.
Let us reserve our planning
Till we join the procession.

(The bard harbingers the king's approach. A short lyric brings him into view. The chiefs join the King. Balogun returns and joins the rest.)

ALAYE:
Blessings to the elders of this great clan.
Blessings to the scions of Adelembade,
To the scions of Osha-Itiletile.
May the head of the crown defend you all.

OTHERS:
Ase.

ALAYE:
You whose blood flows
From the virginity of Erekelayewa,
Our grandmother, mother of Ipenpeju;
Is there any force in this world
To bar you from flapping your wings
Like the bright bird?

OTHERS:
O s'ewo.

ALAYE:
And, like the eagle, we shall soar,
High to the peak of great achievements.
May our fathers make our hopes a reality
And cause greater unity amongst our folds.

OTHERS:
Ase.

ALAYE:
(Paces downstage to peep, returns.)
For the past few days we've been busy
With the reception of Adeboye,
Our illustrious son who will now keep
The sacred grove. Today, the ceremony ends
In the great procession with the white calabash.
And while we prepare for this,
I wish you knew how heavy my heart is

This Proverb

To think that Ifagbaye, the great messenger
Of Orunmila, whose art
Evoked this right image, had to go
To join his fathers so soon
Without waiting to see the ripe fruit
Of a plant he so well nurtured.

    DAKEJA:
Enh, Kabiyesi, Ifagbaye has only changed his form.
He certainly is not dead, so
There is no cause for bitterness.
Let us talk of things of the present, my lord,
And let shadows of the past hold awhile.

    ALAYE:
Dakeja bi eru!
Your words are cracks of thunder.
I shall ever cherish the way they speed me
Into action. Truly,
We shall talk of things of the... **(Peeps.)**
Ahem... **(Song from outside.)** I hear the voice of the village.

    OJOMO:
(Peeps.)
The procession has taken off.

    SAPATIRA:
(Peeps.)
They are heading this way,
Bearing the Hermit shoulder high.

    ALAYE:
Where is my aide? Okitikata!

    OKITIKATA:
Kaabiyesi!

ALAYE:
Open the palace gate. **(Exit Okitikata.)**
The procession will head straight
To the grove from here.

(The song comes alive. A crowd enters from the house. Adeboye is borne shoulder-high for a while, later soft-landed. Heavy instrumentation backs up the song, as each participant illustrates the mood with exciting dance.)

Adeboye oku ewu o
Adeboye, we salute on your safety
Ewu ina, ewu ina
A fire disaster, a fire disaster
Kii p'awodi
Cannot kill the eagle
Awodi oku ewu...
The Eagle, we salute on your safety

PEOPLE:
Kaaabiyesi

ALAYE:
May you live long.
People of Jokoje! **(Now on the dais.)**

ALL:
Ho!

ALAYE:
Sons and daughters of Adelembade.

ALL:
Ho!

ALAYE:
A heart is a heart
Only when it pumps the passion
Of peace and harmony.
A clan is a clan
Only when it lives

This Proverb

In love and harmony.
We are proud winners of these virtues now,
And may such blessings
Continue to come our way.

ALL:
Ase.

ALAYE:
Our purity is no more a thing of doubt
As we have secured a purifier.
Our sacred grove, the sanctified abode
Of our gods and goddesses
Is no more a sham
As we have secured a Hermit.
Here now is Adeboye, the son of Ogbontarigi Umale,
To mount the pivot of our spiritual wheel.
May he be to us a binding force
As were his fathers.

ALL:
Ase. **(Side comments.)**

DAKEJA:
Ase Orisa. But, my Kabiyesi, **(Prostrates and rises.)**
Will it not be proper
If the new Hermit says
A word or two to his people
When the gathering is now full?
He has been here a few days now
And has not uttered beyond the words of greetings
To his laity.
Let him speak to us.
He is no stranger to us. **(Humorous.)**
Even if he is haunted by his city-life mentality,
And the ghosts of book-ideas,
He is still no stranger to us. **(General laughter.)**
Let him speak.

ALAYE:
He will speak, Dakeja.
He will speak
In more than many ways.

BALOGUN:
But, Dakeja, that is not the way
To put forward such a proposal.
This is no time for joking and clowning.
And if anyone should know it,
It is you.

DAKEJA:
You can say whatever you like.
Soon, the sun will set and you and I
Will be left alone to thrash it out.

BALOGUN:
Thrash what out, you...

CROWD:
(Yell at them.) Haa... o to... enough,...

ALAYE:
Eh, the white hen
Is not aware of its eldership.
That is why it is found flapping its plumes
In the dust.

(Sapatira makes a quick exit, known only to Ojomo.)

CROWD:
Uuu – umh! **(A sorry tone.)**

ALAYE:
Adeboye, here now are the people
Whose spongy souls you must make compact.
Would you like to say a word to them
Before the procession takes off?

This Proverb

ADEBOYE:
Since the pillar of my chamber
Has given the option,
I will say a word.
Kabiyesi, the one from whose staff
I take my bearing, my drover,
I pay my respect.
And to the elders, to sons and daughters
Of this great land, I bow my head in humility.
He who taunts at an old man
Should remember that, one day,
His own age, too, will come to be old.
Since, I , Adeboye... or let me say
Since my family will wear the crown
After our mighty one, Alaye,
Shall have taken the big step
To his fathers, I always shudder
At the thought of my causing a set-back
To his successful reign.
This is why I have been so eager to serve him,
To serve Jokoje with all sincerity.
And it is manifested in my whole-hearted acquiescence
In this talk of Hermitship.
The gods have chosen me
With one last thunderous voice
Through the late Ifagbaye.
And I am not hesitant.
It is with a straight choice
That I heed their call.
Let my people, therefore, be assured
That after the gods I chose myself. **(General applause.)**
I left behind me my wife and children,
Alone I left behind me the love I knew, the love I made,
Towards the mystery I do not know,
Towards the mystery I shall be pleased to know.
Let us proceed.

ALAYE:
(**Bearing the white calabash in front of Adeboye**)
Let us proceed
To the sacred grove.

ADEBOYE:
Yes, let us proceed
To the heart of the matter. (**Raises a song.**)

Oyenrenren oloro mi wa o
   Stealthily, the mystique comes.
Ona la
   Road, open!
Mo fe la m'ekun kan
   I'm going to catch a tiger

CHORUS:
Ona la oloro mi wa, ona la
   Road, open! The mystique comes. Open.

(**In a dignified, swaying body-motion, the crowd dances out of the stage, disappearing behind the right wing. Dakeja and Ojomo drop behind, un-noticed by the rest.**)

DAKEJA:
What did you call me for?

OJOMO:
You will soon know.

DAKEJA:
You want me to miss the grand ceremony?
Why did you pinch me and ask me to stay behind?

OJOMO:
I am more eager to watch the ceremony
Than yourself, Dakeja.
The disease that troubles forty
Also troubles four hundred.
The trouble of Aboyade
Is the trouble of all worshippers of Oya.

This Proverb

One who is carrying a load of elephant flesh
Should not dig for a cricket with his foot.

(Sapatira re-appears, bearing the royal staff.)

SAPATIRA:
I have said it.
I have done it.

DAKEJA:
Alaye's royal staff?

OJOMO:
Here it is.

DAKEJA:
What shall we do with it?

SAPATIRA:
We shall hide it.

DAKEJA:
Yes...

ALL:
We shall hide it, we shall hide it,
We shall hide it and tell a lie
Against the city-dweller.
We shall shower a rain of horror on his head.
Then he will know we are not slaves.
We shall not be treated like slaves for his own sake.
Let his book save him now.
Let him take a look at his constitution,
While we find a way out for his constipation.

(The song fades up and down again. Lights fade off.)

ACT TWO : SECOND MOVEMENT

(A roaring voice of **Alaye** is heard before the lights come on. The rumbling sound of drums accompany his raucous voice. Alaye comes into full view in his loin cloth, a beaded bare-chest and a royal cap.)

ALAYE:
What rebel... what rogue was it!

OKITIKATA:
(**Within.**) Kaabiyesi o! (**Appears, panic-stricken.**)

ALAYE:
What beast, I ask you!

OKITIKATA:
What is it Kabiyesi?

ALAYE:
Where is it?
I have searched and searched.
I have peered into nooks
And looked into crannies,
But couldn't find my royal staff...
Go now and wake all the palace attendants,
Wake up my queens, sons and daughters.

OKITIKATA:
It shall be done, Kabiyesi. (**Makes to go.**)

ALAYE:
Come back!
Go to my chiefs.
Tell them I want them here, now.

OKITIKATA:
It shall be done. (**Exit.**)

ALAYE:
Or is it a dream? Could be
Nothing less than a dream
For my symbol of authority
To disappear from me
With my eyes wide-open.

(Palace attendants and wives begin to appear. Chiefs follow.)

This fresh morning,
With its refreshing breeze
Ushering the sun to our clime,
Has been made ominous
Through an act of abomination.

MAADAN:
Kabiyesi o,
My heart shudders
At the urgent call.
May we know...

ALAYE:
Keep your mouth shut, parrot.
Are you not the youngest of my wives?
A teenager with tongue flapping
Like the fang of a viper;
What makes you think
You should be the first to speak
In this assembly?
What makes you think
You are the balm to calm
My heartfelt grief? Parrot...

MOGAJI:
Kabiyesi,
You did not even allow us say
Our words of greetings.

This Proverb

ALAYE:
Yes, Mogaji.
The matter at hand
Is beyond greetings.

MOGAJI:
Ha! No wonder,
No wonder your messenger
Doped me out of the depth of sleep
When I was dreaming with my wife
In my bed.

ALAYE:
Let fathers and mothers and children
Share of the grief. I am
Indifferent to their grumblings.
For their grumblings are but little things
Beside the insult I have received.

BALOGUN:
What insult may this be, my lord.

ALAYE:
Waking up this morning,
I wanted to go to the shrine
To make offering to our fathers
As gratitude for our finding a Hermit.
I wore my ritual robe as usual,
But when I looked behind the door
To pick my royal staff,
IT WAS NOT THERE!

EVERYBODY:
Haaa!

BALOGUN:
This is serious
And... Have you searched?

ALAYE:
Searched every corner!

MOGAJI:
And who could have taken
The king's royal staff?

ALAYE:
That is why I have called you.
If it is anyone in this town
That stole my royal staff,
When such a thief is found,
I will chop off his head
From his body
And curse be unto his family forever.
Mogaji.

MOGAJI:
Kabiyesi.

ALAYE:
Take the town-crier with you,
Go to town and summon all townspeople
To the palace.
Tell them there is fire on the rafter...

(Exit Mogaji. A loud laugh is heard from Dakeja.)

Ah-ah, Dakeja,
Is your head not correct?

DAKEJA:
My head is correct, Kabiyesi. **(The crier's voice heard.)**

ALAYE:
And, does this matter
Call for laughter?

DAKEJA:
It is a bastard that will not laugh
When he has every reason to do so,
Kabiyesi.

(Townsfolks begin to arrive. Mogaji returns.)

This Proverb

SAPATIRA:
Enough of that, Dakeja.
Must you scrub your eldership
On the floor?...

ALAYE:
Leave him...

SAPATIRA:
And, talking about the royal staff;
I saw something like it somewhere,
A fully beaded thing with beaded tassel
And a bulbous silver head. Ojomo...

OJOMO:
Yes, you showed it to me...

SAPATIRA:
Only I cannot remember where.
Remind me.

OJOMO:
Somewhere in the heart
Of the sacred grove.

ALAYE:
Where?

SAPATIRA & OJOMO:
Sacred grove.

DAKEJA:
When I was laughing
Everybody called me a fool.
If I had told you that Adeboye...

CHIEFS:
Adeboye...

DAKEJA:
If I had told you that I saw Adeboye
Stealing the staff away
At twilight yesterday,
Would you still not call me a fool?

BALOGUN:
Impossible.

DAKEJA:
Say what you like.

BALOGUN:
The Hermit is not expected
To leave his grove except
Once in a year. How could he,
On the day of installation...

DAKEJA:
I tell you, we now have a Hermit
Who will be found at disco parties...

ALAYE:
Enough! **(Silence.)**
This is a shocking revelation,
The remedy of which, after investigation,
Requires a fast execution.
Okitikata!

OKITIKATA:
Kabiyesi.

ALAYE:
Go and bring Adeboye. **(Exit Okitikata.)**
True or false,
This story must be followed up.
True of false,
People of Jokoje!

PEOPLE:
Kaabiyesi.

ALAYE:
Go and raid the scared grove.
Search for my royal staff.
If you find it there,
It will be a clue against the alleged impostor.
Go.

PEOPLE:
(Singing as they take their exit .Okitikata returns with Adeboye.)

ADEBOYE:
Kaabiyesi Alaye. **(Silence.)**
It is not customary for the Hermit
To be summoned out of the sanctity of his abode
As you have done.
But since you are the pillar of our house,
Since you are the very staff
With whom we find our bearing,
Here is my presence as you desire.

ALAYE:
Yes, staff Adeboye, staff! I demanded for you.
If there is no cause,
A woman never bears Kumolu.
My royal staff is stolen!

ADEBOYE:
Stolen? How...

ALAYE:
You will know.

(The townspeople are returning. Their song fades up, then down.)

I can hear the voice of the people.

(The folks enter chanting, their leader bearing the staff:
We have found it
We have found it
We have found Opa Oba
We have found it.
The song stops abruptly. There is panic.)

Say ... Is this not my royal staff
I see in your hand?

LEADER:
Kaabiyesi, it is truly your royal staff
I am bearing with my trembling hands.

ALAYE:
And where did you find it. Give me. **(Collects.)**

LEADER:
In the sacred grove, Kabiyesi.

ALAYE:
Where in the sacred grove?

LEADER:
Behind the hut of the new Hermit.

ADEBOYE:
Behind the hut of whom?

LEADER:
Behind your hut, sir,
Hidden under a pile of banana leaves.

ADEBOYE:
Ha-ha ... I didn't ...

WOMAN:
Kabiyesi, it was me
Who used my discretion.
I used my discretion, Kabiyesi.
I went behind his hut and searched and searched.

This Proverb

And, very soon, with these my two eyes
I saw the thing under the banana leaves.
I was afraid to touch it, because I am a woman.
So, I used my discretion
And called this oga because he is a man.
And he pulled it out.
If anybody says we did not find it behind his hut,
Let him come and answer three questions
From me.

ADEBOYE:
I say no... see... what...

ALAYE:
Shut your mouth, you impostor,
Otherwise you will eat
Your pounded yam in yam.

ADEBOYE:
I refuse to shut up, Kabiyesi.
The entrails of a pig
Will not be emptied on my face
With my eyes wide open...

ALAYE:
(**Enraged.**)
Can you hear him still?
He wants to get me mad...

ADEBOYE:
Alaye, this is a...

ALAYE:
I say shut up!

OJOMO:
Enh, Kabiyesi...

ALAYE:
Imagine... And he still has the mouth to... to...

OJOMO:
Kaabiyesi!

ALAYE:
Ehn, I'm hearing you, Ojomo.

OJOMO:
And the elders and people of Jokoje,
If what I will say is wrong,
Please warn me to put my tongue in a lock.
Half of the truth is now revealed.

ADEBOYE:
Half of what truth?
Must you form a jury
Over an unfounded allegation?
Ah-ah, what is the meaning of all this?

OJOMO:
Half of the truth is now revealed.

BALOGUN:
(Exploding in rage. On his feet.)
There is no half of any truth that is revealed.
Look, my stomach is boiling
As I am sitting here.
And, as I am sitting here,
My bottom is cold with surprise.
Kabiyesi, I fear that there is a trap.
We must be very cautious in this case...

ALAYE:
Sit down, Balogun.
I have always respected you
For your wise counseling.
But in this case you have to give room
To better reasoning. Here is one:
Have you often heard Adeboye
Comparing his life to my royal staff?

BALOGUN:
That is out of the way.

This Proverb

ALAYE:
Even on his arrival here, this morning,
This thief still said it...

ADEBOYE:
I am not a thief
I did not...

ALAYE:
Enough, or I feed you to the vultures.
The witch cried yesterday.
The child dies today.
Who does not know
That it was the witch who cried yesterday
That killed the child?

BALOGUN:
The wisdom of our fathers
Is now written upside down.
And this should not happen in my time.
I should not live in a Jokoje
Where trapsters reign supreme.
I fear there is a conspiracy.

DAKEJA/OJOMO/SAPATIRA:
There is no conspiracy.

DAKEJA:
Rather, there is solidarity.
Balogun, must you defend this robber?
Must you defend him
And allow the dignity of our ruler
To be swept under the carpet?

BALOGUN:
I do not call for your appeal, Dakeja.
If you are so hungry for human flesh
You can kill him, kill him,
And eat him up... Kabiyesi, I take my leave.
(Walks out in anger.)

ALAYE:
What! For Balogun to damn my presence
And stage a walkout.
And because of this thief?

ADEBOYE:
Ah, is everybody mad?

EVERYBODY:
What!

DAKEJA:
The bold-face of a swindler!
Put out more pretensions
And let's see where it lands you.
O-O-l-e-e.

WOMAN:
Yes ke. He's an O-L-E-E!

PEOPLE:
O-l-e-e!

ADEBOYE:
Here is the shock!
Here is the shock they speak of;
To wing myself this way
In anticipation of a useful service,
Only to be thus entertained
With a splash of mud!
It's crazy.

SAPATIRA:
Say more. Mr. Philosopher.

ADEBOYE:
I am not a thief
My innocence has robbed me of words.
My consternation wells tears
At the face of this rudeness.

This Proverb

ALAYE:
Half of the truth is revealed.
Now is time for the impostor
To make confession... Abi? Mogaji.

MOGAJI:
Eh, Kabiyesi, I have nothing to say.

SAPATIRA:
Then, let him confess straight.

OJOMO:
Confess your sin.

ADEBOYE:
I am innocent.

ALAYE:
That is ruled out.
Is there anyone to defend him?

MOGAJI:
Ah, the only person who tried to defend him
Has been shunned.
What then is the point
Of any other person defending him
When the King's prejudices are quite clear?

ALAYE:
Mogaji, are you saying I am prejudiced?

MOGAJI:
No, I am not saying so.
But if you are so hungry for human flesh,
If you want to kill him, kill him
And eat him up... Kabiyesi, I take my leave.

ALAYE:
Go if you wish. **(Exit Mogaji.)**
What have I lost by the exit of your betters?
Okitikata.

OKITIKATA:
Kabiyesi.

ALAYE:
Bind him hands and legs.
And in his fetters let him remain
A detainee in my palace
Until I bundle him back to the city
Where he came from.
We refuse to have a thief of a Hermit.
Better no Hermit at all
Than a viper injecting his venom
Into the sanctity of our God-given land.

(Okitikata rushes out through left wing.)

People of Jokoje!

PEOPLE:
Kabiyesi!

ALAYE:
This is the end of the road
For a thief who came in the guise of a messiah.

ADEBOYE:
Oba Alaye,
Worthy of his name
As I used to think,
This act of yours is mean.
I would advise you stop it.

DAKEJA:
See him. He still has the mouth to talk.

ADEBOYE:
And the hands to act, too,
If you try my patience.
I will not be addressed
In such slanderous manner
As the king is doing.
Am I a thief?

PEOPLE:
Yes.

ADEBOYE:
Even you, my people?

PEOPLE:
You have no people here...

ADEBOYE:
Shock!
Wonders will never cease to happen.
Am I so addressed by the people
For whom I sacrifice my family allegiance?
Reason, people, reason;
Could Adeboye have left his luxurious home
In the city
In a bid to steal a mere staff
Of plank and beads?

OJOMO:
But it was found behind your hut.

ADEBOYE:
Treachery has taken the air.
An enemy of mine
Must have done this.

(Enter Okitikata with ropes.)

Hold awhile, you zealot,
Give me space to breath in grief.
And let all of you give me audience
While I land the adze on the roof:
Alaye, we have been friends since our infancy.
So were the father's whose genitals
Spurted out our corporeal being.
Now the raft has drifted apart,
To the mercy of the currents. Therefore,
If you are a true-born
Be not afraid of the current
To which, this moment,

I hand over the movement of your conscience.
It is a mild vituperation,
That must gradually weather
The pedestal of whoever has a hand
In this ignoble plot.
May the person who took the staff
To the sacred grove,
And anyone who has a hand in it
Be rejected by the earth and end up
Scorned in the eye of the sky.
That is the curse. **(Turns to Okitikata.)**
Now, you minion of the law,
Bind me hands and legs
And, in my fetters, let me remain
A detainee in the palace of Alaye,
Until he bundles me back to the city
Where I came from.
Do your work.
(Okitikata binds.)

    ALAYE:
(Laughs in mockery.)
I was almost knocked into sleep
By the stink that came from his mouth.
Lead him away; thief!
Away to the backyard... ole!

    MAN ONE:
I think I pity him. See, poor man.

    MAN TWO:
Until he steals your wife from your underneath.

(As Adeboye is being led away, Alaye is moving out of stage, through left wing. This man raises a chant, chorused by the rest.)

    Ole-ee-ee! Ole-ee-ee
       Rogue, rogue

This Proverb

PEOPLE:
Ekigbe ole mo
  Shout upon the rogue
Ole!
  Rogue!

(Drums come alive to accompany a rowdy chant by the crowd. They all dance away in different directions. Only the scheming trio and Maadan are left.)

MAADAN:
Baba, what were you whispering across
The other time?

DAKEJA:
Nothing much, my daughter,
I was only asking if it wasn't too early
For someone to deprive you of your status as a queen.

MAADAN:
By that you mean?

DAKEJA:
I mean not much, my daughter,
But that I have thought
How disastrous it would have been for you
In the prime of your maidenhood
To have your husband's throne
Usurped by that scoundrel called Adeboye.

MAADAN:
I never imagined he could be so treacherous.

SAPATIRA:
Ha, treachery is his father's first name.
He wanted to bring coup to Jokoje.
Coup. Do you know coup?

MAADAN:
I don't know who is so called.

SAPATIRA:
No wonder. That is why you are sitting down,
Watching the process of the denudation
Of the log you lean upon
Like an ant-infested log of wood.
If there is anyone in this Jokoje
Who should show concern against the threat
Which Adeboye poses to the throne of Alaye,
It is you. Now, tell me, daughter:
Have you had a child for the king?

MAADAN:
No. But we're still trying.

OJOMO:
There you are.

DAKEJA:
You see.
And if the king should be dethroned today,
You will surely lose your enviable position
As the jewel in our eyes. Remember?

MAADAN:
That I know.

DAKEJA:
Therefore let us be united
In our defence of the throne of your husband.
It is with clenched fist
That one strikes the chest, just as
The bunch of broom is best for sweeping.
Let us sweep this house together.
You are the wife to take meals to the prisoner,
So your office serves our interest best.
It has been discovered by the elders
That until the prisoner makes a straight confession
Of his obvious plot against our venerated throne,
His detention is deemed unjust, and
The credibility of Alaye is at stake.
If we must kill a snake,

This Proverb

It must be total.
If we must bring an end to Adeboye's treachery,
Let us not allow him to have a claim
In the eyes of justice. Otherwise,
Sympathy for his cause may breed rebellion,
And the very roof under which we take shelter
May collapse and destroy us all.
Ojomo, Sapatira, I'm I speaking for you?

OJOMO & SAPATIRA:
Yes... Good. Go on.

DAKEJA:
So, his confession is what you must
Persuade him to make
As you carry his food to him
Every morning,
Every afternoon,
Every evening.
Do it like a woman.
Give him all the understanding he needs.
And... if you don't get me clearly,
This is what I mean. **(Jokingly.)**
There are only a few men
Who will not lose their senses
To the warm strokes of a woman's hand...
(Everybody laughs.)

MAADAN:
All you have said is clear to me, and
I shall do my best.

OJOMO:
We shall hide ourselves behind the walls
To catch him with the words.

SAPATIRA:
That we shall do,
As sleek as the worms.

MAADAN:
Ko buru.
I will see to it.
O dabo o.

CHIEFS:
Oo o o. (**Exit Maadan.**)
If we wish it, we will it,
Or else nothing will be here at all.
Slaves of this land,
Elders of this land,
But we refuse to be slaves of this land.
We wish to be elders of this land.
We will be elders of this land,
Or else nothing will be here at all.

DAKEJA:
Listen, my friends,
This wrath destroys even
The petals of innocence.
I keep my form.

OJOMO:
Listen, my friends,
This wrath beclouds even
The sharpest of eyes.
I keep my form.

SAPATIRA:
Listen, my friends,
The wrath pollutes
Most sparkling of waters.
I keep my form.

CHIEFS:
We keep our form.
If we wish it, we will it,
Or else nothing will be here at all.

(**They sing:** 'Awarawa ni Moba...')

ACT TWO : THIRD MOVEMENT

(In the detention yard, Adeboye is chained to a stake.)

        ADEBOYE:
And I am a heir
To the throne that treats me thus?
What explanation can be given
To unravel this mystery?
I have been here three days now,
Flogged and kicked by the whopper,
Asked to confess to a crime
I did not commit.
I look up to the sky and its cloudy shield,
To earth and the gods of this land.
If this yoke is supposed
To be the trial of my time,
Let me bear it calmly.
I am still resolute,
To wait and watch the current.
A little spark might rout the edifice
I have spent years in molding.
So, why not wait and watch.

(Enter Balogun from right wing.)

        BALOGUN:
You are here, my friend?

        ADEBOYE:
Here as you can see.
And the people make trips. . .
To see me in my cage
Like a beast in the zoo.

        BALOGUN:
Bear it like a man this while.
Bear their scornful remarks like a man.
I know the truth will come to light very soon.
I spent the last two days

Communing with my household gods,
And I have sent a curse across
To whoever was responsible
For this foul play.

ADEBOYE:
I praise your efforts, Balogun.
As you can see, I am unruffled.
Only I cannot discuss much about the issue.
I keep my words within myself first.

BALOGUN:
It is the way of a cautious man.
Do well, my friend. I will leave you now.
May the gods protect you.

ADEBOYE:
And you, too.

BALOGUN:
Ase!

(Making to go, meets his son on the way with a drum hung on his shoulder.)

Ah! Ah! Jibola, my son,
Where are you off to?

JIBOLA:
To entertain Papa Adeboye
With the drum he gave to me
When he came to pay you homage.

BALOGUN:
Why?

JIBOLA:
Father, that may be a good way
Of keeping him happy
In this moment of distress.

This Proverb

BALOGUN:
It may be, my son.
I grant you leave to do that.
And when you get back home,
Tell your mother I am holding
An important meeting with the King.

JIBOLA:
Oooo. **(Exit Balogun.)**
Ah – ah – ah! **(Sees a colleague, Baiko, son of Dakeja.)**
Baiko, the devil behind
A maiden's apron.
Are you here with your drum, too?

BAIKO:
Yes, Jibola,
To entertain the good man
Who bought it for me.

JIBOLA:
Let us approach him.
How is your father?

(Enter Dakeja.)

DAKEJA:
What do you want to know
About his father, you brat?
And you, Baiko, have you finished
The work I gave you at home?

BAIKO:
I've done it half-way, father.
I spare half of my time for you
And half for myself.

DAKEJA:
Why?

BAIKO:
Only God knows why.

DAKEJA:
That to your father?

BAIKO:
When my father spares no time at all
For his offspring. Only God knows why
He has carried the job of bearing witness
Against the noblest blood in Jokoje
Solely on his own head.
He has no time for his family.

DAKEJA:
You are a stupid son. Beware!
Beware, or else my fury will fell
A tree and crush you.

BAIKO:
That tree will only do for a faggot, my father.
The torn damask of your shame
Is what I am mending now.
Leave me and go away.

DAKEJA:
Curse be unto you, my son.

BAIKO:
Curse be unto you my father.

(Exit Dakeja.)

Approach, son of Balogun.
Let us go and give honour to who deserves it.
Even if we have no mouth
In the scheme of things,
At least we can take solace in our drums.

(They move towards Adeboye who has started napping.)

JIBOLA:
Papa Deboye! Papa Deboye!!

This Proverb

ADEBOYE:
(Awake.)
Ah, children, blessings.
How are your parents?

JIBOLA:
They are alright.

BAIKO:
My own father is not alright.

ADEBOYE:
Who is your father?
What sickness or ...

BAIKO:
The topic is closed, Papa.
We have come to drum for you.

ADEBOYE:
Commence then, children.
It drives my bile further inward.
Tap the membrane.
It is my pleasure to hear.

(The drumming commences. The chorus joins with mellow lyric in praise of Adeboye. But they were halted by the brusque castigation from Okitikata, now the whopper.)

WHOPPER:
What! Is it because the King
Has ordered for the gate to be opened,
That all willing eyes may come and see
This shameful beast?
Away at once, you little urchins, **(Kicks them.)**
Away to your fathers' houses
Before I wrench your ears.
(Whips them.)

JIBOLA:
Ah - ah! Broda buruku.

BAIKO:
Agba iya.

BOTH:
Oo ni kuure. **(Cursing churlishly, they go out.)**

WHOPPER:
And you thief... **(Whips Adeboye with a horse-whip.)**
Ole! You have the audacity
To call for entertainers...

ADEBOYE:
Ah! Treat me gently... **(In pains.)**

WHOPPER:
Fool...

ADEBOYE:
Not your fault...

(Enter Maadan with a bowl of food.)

MAADAN:
Haa - haaa! Okitikata,
Do it gently.
Don't let him die...

WHOPPER:
I hear you, Maadan.

MAADAN:
Here is your food, Adeboye. **(Sets the food before him.)**
I'm going for water. **(Exit Maadan.)**
(Adeboye starts to eat.)

WHOPPER:
Stop eating. Give me that food.
I need it more than you.
I do the beating ...
I waste more energy.

Give me the food, thief.
(He rushes it down his gullet.)

ADEBOYE:
But why must you deprive me
Of this only privilege?

WHOPPER:
Only God knows why. **(Kicks Adeboye. Maadan returns catching Okitikata in the act.)**

MAADAN:
Ah-ah! Gently Okitikata!
Has he finished eating? So fast?
Papa, do you need more?

ADEBOYE:
I can't say I don't.

MAADAN:
I will get more.
Okitikata, go and break me some firewood.
I will be doing more cooking very soon.

OKITIKATA:
Alright Maadan. **(Exit Okitikata.)**

MAADAN:
Drink water. **(Hands him the cup.)**

ADEBOYE:
Thank you. **(Drinks.)** Thanks.

MAADAN:
Ehen, now Papa Adeboye,
For the past two days,
I've been trying to get the facts out of you.
But you remain adamant.
Believe me,
If you truly confess,
I will plead on your behalf,
Plead on my two knees

That you be forgiven.

ADEBOYE:
What is there to confess
In a crime you do not commit, daughter?
Have I not said enough?
Or are you asking me to please you
By cutting my own throat
For no just cause?

MAADAN:
Come, be not annoyed with me. **(Caressing.)**

ADEBOYE:
What did you do that for?

MAADAN:
A woman's breast is the home of feelings.
I pity you, my bosom pities you. Come.
Defy not the appeal from the depth
Of my solicitude... **(Caressing.)**
I do not wish...

ADEBOYE:
(Trying to resist.)
Look, I will not allow myself
To be thus used in a bid to get
What is not there.
How many words will fill a basket?
For the past two days, we have been on it.
Now you see your effort ending in futility
And you change to the most ignoble tactics.
Leave me.

(Dakeja, Ojommo and Sapatira enter quietly from left wing, watch intently, withdraw via same. While they do this, Maadan speaks on.)

MAADAN:
It is not easy to leave you.
Look at my eyes and let the words come out.
Do not hide them from me.

This Proverb

I mean no harm. **(Hugs.)**

    ADEBOYE:
Perhaps you have been told
That it is the meticulous killer of the ant
That gets it's entrails.
Here you miss it, my daughter.
I am a stump of wood
Severed from the roots.
I have no vessels.
I have no intestine.

    MAADAN:
But you have words. **(Giggles and lunges herself amorously on him.)**
You have words shielded by vanity.

(At this point, Alaye arrives at the spot with Dakeja, Ojomo and Sapatira. They watch perturbed.)

Is this the kind of husband
You will make to palace queens
When Alaye shall have climbed the rafter?

(Alaye cuts in fiercely. Removes and wears back his crown.)

    ALAYE:
There he is now,
Too eager to be there.
He stole my staff. Now,
There he is, making love to my own wife.
Love to my wife?
Adeboye! Maadan!

(The victims are shocked. Alaye boils.)

Dakeja!

    DAKEJA:
I'm happy we now see it
With our own eyes.

ALAYE:
Sapatira!

SAPATIRA:
The eyes of a man
Are never known to deceive him.

ALAYE:
Ojomo!

OJOMO:
Adeboye!

ADEBOYE:
From frying-pan to fire.
Believe me ...

ALAYE:
Making love to my own wife?
This brute? H-e-e-e-e-e-e-y!
My blood is hot, my eyes are dazed.
The world will know this. **(Approaches Adeboye.)**
Listen, you fornicator,
Your cup is replete with shame.
And today, this very day,
I will empty its sour fluid
Where it rightly belongs.
(Turns to Maadan, strikes her with his staff.)
And you witch, p-r-o-s-t-i-t-u-t-e!
Get inside! I will come and land my axe on you.

ADEBOYE:
Alaye, be scrupulous, please.
She it was who tried to move.

ALAYE:
She will move you yet,
And move you out of here.
She will move you to the darkness you seek,
Out of the sight of life.
She still will move you to the evil forest
Where you rightly belong.

This Proverb

Go at once, Sapatira!
Take my town crier with you,
And call the people of Jokoje here again.
We must call them here again and again
To bear witness to the shame of our time,
The bane of our clime. **(Exit Sapatira.)**

    ADEBOYE:
Oba Alaye, come. Let me kneel at your feet
And tell you that these things,
That these crimes are still a mystery to me.
I vouch, the agents of darkness are at work.
If they are not human, they are more than human.
But I cannot point out which is which.
I only find myself here or there
Like a feather in the wind.
And I fear to fight the wind.
I fear the wind.
Lest it should blow more blusterous
And empty sand in innocent eyes.

    ALAYE:
The sand will be blown in your eyes
And in your eyes alone.
Plead no more, as I have seen
With my naked eyes,
Your naked, shameful being.

    ADEBOYE:
Could the trust of past years
Not make you rethink?

(Townfolks arrive. Mogaji leads them.)

    ALAYE:
Whoever can say,
 'This is the colour of the chameleon today ',
Let him keep trusting you.

    MOGAJI:
What is the trouble again?

ALAYE:
Mogaji, yesterday, because of this fool,
You called me a cannibal.
Would you believe now
That I caught him making love to Maadan,
My youngest wife, a while ago?

PEOPLE:
Eewoh!

WOMAN:
This man; ah- ah,
Something must be pushing him.

LEADER:
That is the way of the city.
I hear anybody has intercourse with just anybody.
Even brothers will not mind
To have intercourse with their own sisters.

DAKEJA:
Never in Jokoje, never.
Kabiyesi, did you hear
What this gentleman said?

ALAYE:
What?

DAKEJA:
He said that in the city
Brothers will not mind to copulate
With their sisters.

(The people are alarmed.)

Look, Adeboye,
If that is what you want to import
Into this peaceful community,
We shall resist it.
Our gods and ancestors shall resist it.
The earth and the sky shall resist it.

This Proverb

ADEBOYE:
Dakeja.

DAKEJA:
That is my name.
What have you got to say?
What have you got to say
When you have been caught?

ADEBOYE:
This is the second time
You are leading a frontal attack
In a bid top disrepute me.

OJOMO:
Hear him.
Do you have any reputation?

ADEBOYE:
Shall I begin to see you
In another light?

DAKEJA:
See me in whatever light you may wish.

ADEBOYE:
Your opposition is too sharp.

DAKEJA:
Eh! A belated cry on the thief
Opportunes him to cry on the owner.
Agbere...

ALAYE:
Enough! We waste words,
This is not a meeting of parrots.
Let our actions speak for us.

DAKEJA:
I'm sorry, Kabiyesi.

ALAYE:
People of Jokoje!

PEOPLE:
Kabiyesi.

ALAYE:
This is the face of Adeboye;
One who was once held in high esteem,
But has now descended with self-debasement
To the platform of screes.
Judgement shall be passed here and now.
The wrath of the lion will fall.
It is the man who insults the King
That dies by the sword of the King.

OJOMO:
Agboye!

PEOPLE:
Agboye!

ALAYE:
Therefore, listen to my proclamation.
This very day, Adeboye,
The son of Ogbontarigi Umale,
Is banished from this town for seven years.
His home shall be the evil forest.
There in the evil forest, let him be haunted
By the witches.
Let him be entertained
With the daemonic dance of imps.
A leper is cast out until he is healed.
We cast you out, Adeboye.

ADEBOYE:
A request, if the gate of mercy is barred.
Let me send a message to my wife and children.

ALAYE:
You're no more of this world
And you are not granted the chance

This Proverb

To communicate with this world.
You have soiled the harmony of this world
And your excommunication is total.
Leave your wife and children to lead their lives,
And go your way into the heart of ignominy.

ADEBOYE:
Not even a word to them?

ALAYE:
Not a word.
Okitikata!

OKITIKATA:
Kabiyesi.

ALAYE:
Unbind his legs
And lead him to the outskirts
Of the evil forest. Leave him there
And return to us. **(Exit Alaye.)**

OKITIKATA:
Up fool. **(Raises a chant.)**
Ole to gbe kakaaki oba
   A rogue that steals the King's trumpet;
Nibo ni'o ti fun?
   Where will he perform with it?
Ole to fe gba'yawo oba
   A rogue trying to snatch the King's wife;
Nibo ni'o ti se?
   Where is he going to do it?

(The people join briefly as Adeboye is being whipped off by his escort, until Baiko stops them with a prolonged shout.)

BAIKO:
No-o-o-o-o-o-o-o-o-o!
People of Jokoje!
Has it ever happened like this before?
You sing, you chant, you dance

Without waiting to reason once.
Has it ever happened like this before?
What is justice without a proper trial?
How can the accuser be the judge?
Straight, one who has been our hero
Is now declared a renegade.
And you say yes
Without waiting to reason once.

OJOMO:
Dakeja! Is that not your son?

DAKEJA:
A foolish son. I have disowned him.

BAIKO:
I hear my father's voice.

DAKEJA:
Not your father's.
If you dare call me your father,
You die. **(Attacks his son.)**

BAIKO:
See him ... see him ...

(The voices of pacifists rise. Lights fade out on the scuffle.)

ACT TWO : FOURTH MOVEMENT

(Dark stage.)

        LEAD:
Ona han o
   Where is the route?
Ona yi han o
   Where is this route?
Ekun mi r'oko o
   The tiger is heading to the bush

        CHORUS:
Ona tororo f'eju no
   Let the footpath broaden
Wa d'ona ragbaja
   And become a highway
Ona la
   Let the road widen
Ekun mi b'ode o
   The tiger is heading back home

        LEAD:
Ekun mi r'oko
   The tiger is heading to the bush

        CHORUS:
Ona la
   Let the road widen
Ekun mi r'oko o
   The tiger is heading to the bush

        LEAD:
Ekun mi b'ode
   The tiger is heading back home

        CHORUS:
Ona la
   Let the road open
Ekun mi b'ode o...
   The tiger is heading back home...

(This is sung over three rounds. Okitikata's voice cracks in like thunder. He is whip-lashing Adeboye. The stage is dark throughout.)

OKITIKATA:
We are in the evil forest.

(Weird voices like shrieks and quacks are accompanied by rolling drum sounds.)

Adeboye!

VOICES:
(Weird.) A-d-e-b-o-y-e!

ADEBOYE:
Okitikata, this place is dark and dreadful.
Are you leaving me here?
Stay with me for a while, friend.

OKITIKATA:
This is a place for sinners,
Not for me.
Adeboye, I must leave you,
As my king and master has commanded.
But I shall endeavour, despite my hurry,
To drop you one last word.
Are you listening to me?

ADEBOYE:
I hear your voice rumbling like this darkness.

OKITIKATA:
And can you see my face?

ADEBOYE:
I see no face except the face of darkness.
But speak on. It gives me consolation.

This Proverb

OKITIKATA:
Adeboye, I have been unkind to you.
I know I have been cruel,
But I ask for your forgiveness.
For I am nothing but an automaton
In the hands of the law.
My private reason tells me you are innocent.
My public reason compels me to acknowledge your guilt.
This is the life I lead;
To know and pretend not to know.
And I plead for your forgiveness.
Here, I undress myself before you.
It will be my last respect.
When you return to Jokoje,
You will not meet me there.
For I am going to another country
Where my conscience will be free.

ADEBOYE:
Okitikata,
I bless you, plead no more.
Put on your clothes...
Hark!

VOICES:
Elegbara o ho!
Elegbara o ho!
Elegbara o ho!
Elegbara o ho!

ADEBOYE:
What voices are those?

OKITIKATA:
Must be the children of Esu Elagbara.
Release me Adeboye...

ADEBOYE:
Good friend, good-bye.

(Exit Okitikata as Esu Elegbara rushes in with fire on his head. Moving trees enter.)

ELEGBARA:
Hoo-haaa! **(Voice uncanny.)**
A new-comer. Who is he?
Heeeeiyah!

ELEGBARA AND VOICES:
Talk!

ADEBOYE:
Help ... ah... help... ah...

ELEGBARA AND VOICES:
Talk!

ADEBOYE:
I will talk, I...

ELEGBARA:
What's your name?

ADEBOYE:
Adeboye.

ELEGBARA:
From where?

ADEBOYE:
Banished from Jokoje.

ELEGBARA:
Ha-a-a! Omo eniyan,
I smell no fault in you.
I smell no fault at all.
But as you have seen me,
The rain comes down.
I am the life of death.
This is the label with which you are admitted.
This is the emblem of your initiation.
After your initiation,

This Proverb

You will be free to dance with my imps,
To dine with my vultures
And hunt with my pythons.
You will be free to drum with my apes.
You are in the world of the downing.
Bear it so and it pleases me.
Heiya-a-a-ah!

(Whisks Adeboye out. The chant of Elegbara is repeated again over a number of rounds.)

ACT THREE : FIRST MOVEMENT

(Evil Forest; purely animistic setting. Adeboye's hut Centre – Stage surrounded by bough-bearing transfixed human figures posing in various ways. Their looks are weird. Adeboye is seen returning after taking a bath.)

ADEBOYE:
Here where we are downing
The cock never crows.
Here, where we are downing,
Is the heart of fear.
I have been here three months
And I've never heard the voice of mirth.
There is no cause for joy here.
Alas! There is no cause for sadness.
For to be joyous is to be sad.
It is with tears that we flash our smile.

SPIRITS OF THE TREES:
(Murmur, they shake their boughs.)

ADEBOYE:
Dear animist souls
Which interpose between us and our fates,
I have woken up again this night.
Oh! Woken to your eternal night,
And by my sworn oath to Elegbara,
I should break kola on your earth
To immunize myself against life's tremors.
Here is your kola.

SPIRITS OF THE TREES:
(Murmur. They shake their boughs.)

ADEBOYE:
I should pour wine.
Here is your wine.

SPIRITS OF THE TREES:
(Murmur. They shake their boughs.)

ADEBOYE:
You have eaten and you have drunk.
Now turn your face and look at me.
You petrified demons of this heart,
Behold. Here is a man cast away
By the people whose welfare he sought to protect.
I am no wizard. I am no villain.
I am not in the least a rebel to my clan.
But the big rain has fallen... I see something;
The running water has lifted the rock from its cradle.
The blusterous wind is blowing.
Ha! And trees and shrubs are trembling.
See them, see them! Gaze upon earth
And look at the sky; all whirling with my cyclone,
Whirling, muddling up my imagination. Enh?
You castaway spirits; can't you offer
Something different from peace or violence?
Ohooo! Here where we are downing
There is no rest, but palpitation.
Let it palpitate, then. Do you object?
Let it palpitate with a touch of the daemon.
Let my volcano rave in the sordid dance of the daemon.
(He dances in a wild, distorted manner.)
Dance, daemon! Dance in your wild transmogrification
And shout your hollah
To your craggy comrades.
(Goes to sit. Wipes sweat.)
Be exactly where your fate has driven you,
But celebrate.
Exactly here, and celebrate.
Even here on this bestial platform,
I will celebrate my degeneration.
(He sings.)

This Proverb

LEAD:
Abo mi d'odun eje o
  My return is in the seventh year

CHORUS:
Odun eje
  Seventh year

LEAD:
Abo mi d'odun eje o
  My return is in the seventh year

CHORUS:
Odun eje
  Seventh year

LEAD:
Igbo nla, igbo ewu
  Massive forest, dreadful forest

CHORUS:
Odun eje
  Seventh year

LEAD:
Ikoko ni mo nwo
  I glance at an angle of it

CHORUS:
Odun eje...
  Seventh year...

(Exit Adeboye with the moving trees. Enter Dakeja, Ojomo and Sapatira, masked.)

SAPATIRA:
Where is he?
Let him come down for the final round.

OJOMO:
Let him come down,
To worse than the den.

DAKEJA:
He owes us nothing that he must pay.

OJOMO:
We owe him nothing that we must pay.

SAPATIRA:
But he has answers to answer.

DAKEJA:
Our answers shall be his questions.

OJOMO:
Why must he buy his laurels
With our sweat?

CHIEFS:
Are we his beasts of burden?

DAKEJA:
Emeralds glitter on the body of a horse.

SAPATIRA:
What of the pain he bears
Bearing his master?

OJOMO:
Let the master and his beast
Swap places for once.

SAPATIRA:
Let the horse become the rider.

DAKEJA:
And the rider the horse.

CHIEFS:
Over the body of Adeboye
At least we shall triumph.

OJOMO:
I shall make him walk on four.

SAPATIRA:
I shall make him wear the skin of a beast.

DAKEJA:
And I shall make him bleat like a sheep.
His tongue must be sealed,
For nobody must relate
This story of our triumph.
This history of our triumph
No history must recall.

CHIEFS:
Where is he now?
War on Adeboye!
Let him come down
From evil to evil.
Let him come down
And bear the mark of our spleen.
W-A-A-R-R!

(Their war-cry is accompanied by a deep rolling of the drums. Adeboye's song, 'Abo mi d'odun eje' is heard again. He is returning with the moving trees.)

DAKEJA:
Halt! **(The trees settle back to their initial positions. Adeboye stares wildly.)**
You have the audacity
To revel in your damnation?
Even here where you should be sober?

ADEBOYE:
You phantom beings,
I am one of you already,
So you can't scare me.
Away and leave me to my revelling!

SAPATIRA:
Today, Adeboye, you end the course
Of the living.

OJOMO:
Take this blow and be on four.

(Smacks Adeboye who drops on the ground instantly, a quadruped, jumping like a cat.)

ADEBOYE:
You phantom beings, don't tempt me.
I will be more than wild.

SAPATIRA:
Here! Another mark!!

(Adeboye rolls on the ground, his skin transformed to that of a beast.)

ADEBOYE:
Tempt me no further,
Or I'll prove myself.
If you come any closer,
I will use my machete...

(The three chiefs draw their machetes. Darkness.)

In the name of Elegbara
Who protects this forest you call evil,
I charge you not to commit
An abomination.

CHIEFS:
We do not belong to Elegbara.

ADEBOYE:
And I protect his interest.

(He attacks. Enter Elegbara with bold gestures. The forest shakes as the chiefs combat Adeboye in what appears like an epic battle. All this while, Elegbara's hand is raised and is not dropped until Adeboye has accomplished his mission, felling the three chiefs. The forest is still.)

This Proverb

ELEGBARA:
I protect those who belong to me. **(Exit. Chorus chants 'Elegbara o...' as he departs.)**

ADEBOYE:
He protects those who belong to him.
Even the daemons protect their comrades.
I have seen it otherwise in Jokoje.
And here, I seem fulfilled
In the world of the opposites.
(He makes to stand on his feet. It is futile.)
What? I cannot stand on my feet!
(Tries to pull off the fur, but it is stuck.)
And the skin of a beast my permanent apparel?
I have been charmed. Wonder!
Do I still speak in your language?
See what these strangers have made of me.
They deserve more than death. You...
Transform me into this monstrosity?
Ha! May you be rejected by the earth
And your souls scorned in the eye of the sky.
(He draws closer, grabs the head of one of the dead chiefs, shakes it angrily, clutching his fingers to the corpse's hairs.)
Even in your death, you will taste of my wrath.
(Shocked as the dead man's mask is ripped off.)
What? Fake, fake! I thought they were ghommids.
Whose face? Ha, my own clansman, Sapatira.
I have tried and tried to shield myself from this reality.
But it comes. It comes. Who's this? **(Rips.)**
Ha, Dakeja! I can guess the third – Ojomo.
Yes. **(Rips.)** Ehen.
(Suddenly, his voice turns raucous, metallic, though audible.)
It is revealed. See them.
I suspected their machination.
But who was I to act on mere suspicion?
My education abhorred that,
So I kept my quiet.
I only hissed and crawled on like a snail.
Still, I arrive.

I have crawled down the slope and arrived,
Arrived to see the scheme of Alaye and his aides.
These three have tasted of retribution.
It is left for their master, now,
To lick the blade of my razor.
I will leave these to rot here,
Let their carcasses be fodder for monsters
And maggots. Let the vultures peck at their flesh.
And while they rot, I will arm myself
With charm and potions.
I will seek redress with the gods.
I must return to Jokoje to unseat that tyrant
Who makes a travesty of the title Alaye.
I will unseat him and take my father's throne.
Let the beast rule over humans no more,
Catalysing the bestialising of humans.
I will return to recapture the purity
On which my land was founded.

(Strange beasts are seen rushing in to devour the bodies of the dead chiefs.)

There is a feast for you mates.
It takes the living to know how it tastes.
Go on with your supping hounds.
Go on with the ritual of my unbecoming.
(Lights out.)

ACT THREE : SECOND MOVEMENT

(Palace. Balogun and Mogaji are seated, meditating. Mogaji breaks the silence.)

    MOGAJI:
Three months now,
And we have not seen Ojomo.
We have not seen Sapatira.
We have not seen Dakeja.
Even Okitikata has disappeared.

    BALOGUN:
Where could they be?
That's the question.

    MOGAJI:
No one knows where they could be.
And Alaye is worried.
Over seven times he has fallen into nightmare
In the dead of the nights.
His attendants say the pressure of his blood and his fever
Have sent him into the world of the unconscious
More than three times. **(Pause.)**
His wives say he refused to eat.

    BALOGUN:
Mogaji, these things are beyond me.
And I reckon they have to do
With the banishment of Adeboye.
You know as much as I do
That there was no clear cause for his banishment.
He was a well-bred son of the soil
Whose love for his people was as warm as the soil itself.
How could he then...
How could he turn around
To cast off his robe of damask
For the wastrel of a lunatic.
I asked for an explanation, nobody gave one.

But the accuser went on,
Throwing missiles of hate
Against the bringer of good life.
And so we have arrived at the nodal point of puzzles.
We have trodden to the crossroads,
On the maze of self-rejection.
The whole town is gripped
With ugly anticipations,
Haunted by uncertainties
And the mysteries of living.
Adeboye is cast off like a louse.
Ojomo has disappeared.
Sapatira is missing.
Dakeja is nowhere to be found.

    BOTH:
Mothers fear and fathers fear.
Farmers forget their farms awhile.
The earth has no yield.
The sky is quiet.
The mind of man is caught with grief.
There will be an answer, I know.
There must be an answer
To these strange happenings.

(A feminine voice cries from within. Maadan's voice. She enters, trembling.)

    MAADAN:
Oba w'aja o...
Oba w'aja o...

    BALOGUN:
Eh, what?

    MAADAN:
Oba w'ajaaaaaa...

    MOGAJI:
Enh, how?

MAADAN:
He was just seeing me
When he suddenly collapsed.
A little drop and his manhood went soft.
He was seeing me
And he collapsed.
I called him, but he didn't answer.
He did not answer...

BALOGUN:
Mogaji, stay here.
Let me go in and see. **(Exit.)**

MOGAJI:
Did you touch his body?

MAADAN:
His body was cold.
We had only gone a little way
When he suddenly gave up...
(Enter Balogun.)

MOGAJI:
How?

BALOGUN:
Go inside, woman.
Tell it to no one yet.

MOGAJI:
Then, it is true.

BALOGUN:
He should not have gone into that woman
At this time of his sickness.
Oh, oh, oh Alaye;
There he was, stiff like a rock
In his nudity,
His probing eyes wide open
As if he wants to see
How these strange happenings
Will end. But he has climbed the rafter.

We it is who will clear the dung.

MOGAJI:
And the woman?

BALOGUN:
I have not forgotten.
She has to go with him.
She has seen what she should not have seen.
The death of a king is a sight too much
For the eyes of a woman.

MOGAJI:
But I am beginning to think.

BALOGUN:
Think what?

MOGAJI:
That Maadan should live.
She may be carrying a child in her womb.
If not, at least these times demand
That we encourage the fulfilment of life;
That we allow for continuity.
Let her be fulfilled
And other stories be framed
Sorrounding the transition of Alaye.

BALOGUN:
Your words are wise, Mogaji.
Besides, I fear, now, to dabble into
The rites of death.
Let us, at once, settle the dead
And open a gate for the future.
Let us summon the elders
For the funeral rites.

MOGAJI:
Yes.
And, afterwards, we shall go
For the regent.

This Proverb

BALOGUN:
Yes, that must be Adewale, the son of Adeboye.

MOGAJI:
Yes, it must be Adewale,
Since his father is still stuck
In the evil forest.

BALOGUN:
But I fear; Adewale may refuse
On grounds of age.

MOGAJI:
Yes, he is too young, but
Adewale will not refuse.
His father, Adeboye
Did not refuse to be the Hermit.
And it is one's father
That one resembles.
There is no rebellion
In the blood of the children
Of Ogbontarigi Umale.
So, Adewale will not refuse.

BALOGUN:
It is so to be hoped.
Let us go now with our woe-betiden heads
To tell Jokoje the terrible news.

BOTH:
Let us go to the elders.
Let us go to the youths.
Let us go to the people of Jokoje.
And tear their ears
With the sad tones of our drums.

(A song is raised backstage as they take their exit.)

O lo o 'Male wa
   Our masquerade is gone
Iyo-yo-yo
O lo o 'Male wa
   Our masquerade is gone
Iyo-yo-yo
Ekun yi ma pade o
   This door is shut
Iyo-yo-yo
Okukun ma su miwa o
   Darkness is hovering
Iyo-yo-yo
Ona yi ma ti di o
   This road is blocked
Iyo-yo-yo
O lo o 'Male wa
   Our masquerade is gone
Iyo-yo-yo
   Iyo-yo-yo

(Lights fade off.)

ACT THREE : THIRD MOVEMENT

(Evil forest. Adeboye has just finished a meal. He is packing his belongings, just a selection of necessary personal effects. He ends it all by filing his machete.)

          ADEBOYE:
A speedy execution
Now that I am charged.
Now that I am charged,
The head of Jokoje will fall.
I see it clearly;
There will be a change.
There will be a change.
With my hands I will bring about the change.
Enough of the rule of terror
Fuelled by sycophantic upstarts.
Now that I have realised there's been a plot,
I must quell the fire of the plot.
It is sheer forbearance that rules the mind of a cow.
A knife does no good on the throat.
The bull will now kick. Let the bludgeon fall.
Let him land his hoof on the skull of Alaye.
(Moves towards the skeletons – the remains of Dakeja, Ojomo and Sapatira.)
He must come to join these fools,
To be thus rejected by the earth and the sky.
(Carries his sack. Hangs his machete on his shoulder.)
I go now, you spirits that guard this forest.
The world of humans calls me
To the ritual of hate.
True, my exit will make you weaker,
Yet you know as I do
That I do not belong here.
I have stayed one full year with you.
Allow me now to go to where I truly belong.
Green spirits of the trees!
Black spirits of the earth!

Red spirits of fire!
Blue spirits of the waters and the skies!
I pay my respect as due.
And here, too, I involve the spirit of my fathers
To aid me in this mission of hate.
The son of a warrior never skulks in the frontier of war.
The son of Ogbontarigi Umale
Will not shed the leaves of gallantry
And allow the reign of slimy goblins.

    VOICES:
Go.

    ADEBOYE:
Yes, I go.

    VOICES:
Go.

    ADEBOYE:
To Jokoje I proceed.

    VOICES:
Go.

    ADEBOYE:
I have been asked by spirits and gods.
And as I go, they must go with me.
My fulfilment must be seen by man and more than man,
Even by the daemons of this dire forest,
As a landmark in the modelling of man.

(Sings.)

    LEAD
Ogbontarogi Umale o
    The majestic masquerade

    CHORUS
Mo dupe
    I am thankful

This Proverb

LEAD
Oro inu iroko o
  Spirit of the Iroko tree

CHORUS
E ma se o
  I am grateful

LEAD
Orisa abule yeye mi o
  Gods of my mother's village

CHORUS
Sara o
  I hail you

LEAD
Anjonu abule baba mi o
  Spirits in my father's village

CHORUS
Baba yeeee
  I bow to fatherhood

LEAD
T'o tun s'eyin l'o ran mi o
  And, since I am sent by you

CHORUS
Iba o, Iba o
  I pay homage, I pay homage

LEAD
T'o tun s'eyin l'o ran mi o
  Since I am sent by you

CHORUS
Iba o, iba o...
  I pay homage, I pay homage...

(Exit as the Lights fade off.)

CONCLUSION

(Palace. Adewale, the son of Adeboye has been installed as the Regent of Jokoje, to stand in for his father until he returns from his penal habitation in the evil forest and on the condition that he is divinely absolved and cleansed to assume Kingship. But the young man is embattled with the upheaval in the town, instigated by a group of agitated youths led by Baiko. The Regent is pensive.)

ADEWALE:
Jokoje has asked me to be the Regent
Until my father is found, and
I have consented.
But, tell me, is there no one in Jokoje
To tell me the whereabouts of my father?
Where is your Hermit? Where is my father?

BALOGUN:
Kabiyesi!
In the face of the truth let no man shudder.
I shall tell what my eyes have seen.
I can see the son of Dakeja is here.
Let him not feel offended
When I tell Kabiyesi
That his father and Ojomo and Sapatira
Plotted against Adeboye.

BAIKO:
I take no offence.
I knew it all the time.
Was it not in the presence of the whole town
That I wrestled with my father?
Was it not for the same cause?
It was for my father's machination
That Alaye, our former ruler, banished Adeboye,
The father of our present ruler
To the evil forest for seven years.

ADEWALE:
Evil forest?

BAIKO:
Yes, evil forest **(Exit Adewale distressed.)**

BALOGUN:
Baiko, your mouth is too wide.
You shouldn't have broken it like that.

BAIKO:
Let us break it, Baba.
Let us break it and let everybody know.

MOGAJI:
Let him use his youthful courage
To speed things up, Balogun.
Is there any use in sniffing around the calabash?
If the calabash faces downwards
We open it,
If it refuses to open...

MOGAJI & BAIKO:
We break it!

BAIKO:
Let it crack and thunder.
Let destruction go haywire.
There are more wicked ones in Jokoje
Than my father and his clique.
And they shall taste of fire.

BALOGUN:
What is the sermon you're preaching, Baiko?

BAIKO:
Baba, you will see
When it begins to happen.
One thing I want to assure you
Is that the legs of the wicked ones
Will be swept clean from Jokoje.
I have been in the fight

This Proverb

Since I grew my wisdom teeth.
It was for this cause
That I cursed my own father.
And if I shall die for this cause,
Let me die.

MOGAJI:
Must you carry the load of the town
On your own head?

BAIKO:
The load of this town is the load of Adewale.
Adewale is my friend.
The load of Adewale is my load.
And I must bear it.
Today I shall burn down the house of my father.
I shall burn down the house of Sapatira.
I shall burn down the house of Ojomo
And all the other rebels lurking
Around the corners of Jokoje.
They have sown a bad seed for the future.
And they must taste
Of what grows out of it.
At once, Jibola, let us go.
Let's gather our age-mates
To annihilate the dark faces of wicked ones.

(Baiko, JIbola and mates take their exit.)

BALOGUN:
See. Son of a bastard;
He has taken my own son
Along with him.
Jibola! Jibola!!... Gone.
Mogaji, I am hanging loose in the void.
I am hanging more loose than the lost.

MOGAJI:
My throat is smothered.
I can't breathe.

(Enter Adewale.)

ADEWALE:
Poor remains of elders,
I have broken the news to Morola, my mother.
It is her tears that drive me back to you.
The palace is dark with grief.
I would appeal that you leave me for now.

(Chant Within: DAKEJA IKU O...)

What noise is that?

BALOGUN:
Baiko is calling for
A solidarity of youths.

ADEWALE:
They are your children.
Go and keep them calm.
Leave me alone for a while, chiefs.
I want to think.

MOGAJI:
Toh! We shall come again tomorrow morning.
Good night.

ADEWALE:
Good night.

(Chiefs take their exit, then rush back.)

BALOGUN:
Heh!
Baiko is already setting
The town ablaze.

MOGAJI:
Kabiyesi, we cannot leave
This palace yet.
It is not safe.

ADEWALE:
Away at once and smell your own stool.

This Proverb

(Rioters enter, chiefs escape through another direction.)

Baiko, I did not send you to do this.

BAIKO:
Dear Regent,
You did not send me.
I have sent myself.

ADEWALE:
I am still thinking of
How to bring my father back.

BAIKO:
Your father will be brought back
To the throne of his fathers.
But, before he returns,
Let the blood of his adversaries flow.
We are heading now to my father's house.
Follow, my people.

(Chanting, Rioters take their exit.)

ADEWALE:
Come back, come back... Baiko **(Exit.)**

(Enter Balogun and Mogaji.)

BALOGUN:
What you said is correct.
There is no need for all this at all.
Since the enemies of Adeboye are gone,
Let his son bring his father back to the throne.
And there is peace.

MOGAJI:
Simple!
And I don't think
Adewale is taking it as seriously
As Baiko is trying to make us believe.
Get me clearly, Balogun.

Since Adewale took over the throne
As the regent of Jokoje,
Every woman in the palace is pregnant
Except his mother. Adewale is not making
A mountain out of this problem like his friends.
Even when we weep
We still maintain a clear vision.
I don't want to carry
Unnecessary trouble on my head.
Let Adewale call Baiko to order.
Everything should be peaceful by now.
Let's go and tell him that. O ya!

BALOGUN:
O ya! Let's go.

(They encounter the rioters who chase them out. Enter Adewale.)

ADEWALE:
I am hopeless.
I lose my father.
My mother is in distress.
And here I am.
Ruling over a turbulent people.

(Sits to meditate. Enter Adeboye from behind Adewale.)

ADEBOYE:
There, the fiend.
Here, I come to take your life.
I can see the town on tumult,
As a prelude to the final act.
I shall be the final actor.
Alaye, it is not seven years yet,
But I have returned.
Returned to take my father's throne,
And restore peace, perfect peace to Jokoje.
(Moves nearer to Adewale. Strikes.)
There!

ADEWALE:
(Drops dead.)
They betray the father
And kill the son... They ...

ADEBOYE:
(Going the opposite direction.)
Rejoice, everyone, rejoice.
Where are the sons and daughters of this land?
Rejoice at your triumph.

(Enter Morola.)

MOROLA:
What wailing? What cry? Where from?
I heard it... ah! My son, my son...
And what monster is this?

ADEBOYE:
(Turns around.)
Monster? Ah! Morola!
Is this not Morola, my wife?
What do you want in the palace of Alaye?

MOROLA:
Who?

ADEBOYE:
Adeboye your husband.

MOROLA:
Adeboye, did you kill my son?

ADEBOYE:
Your son?

MOROLA:
Did you kill Adewale, your son?
Did you kill our son?
E gba mi ooooo...

(Drums. Exit Morola, screaming in horror.)

ADEBOYE:
Adewale...
(Moves to the corpse.)
Ha-aah! Terror, grip me more,
But wake my poor boy.
Breathe again poor boy. And
Let me toy with your tender hands...

(Enter Balogun and Mogaji.)

MOGAJI:
What cry again?

BALOGUN:
I heard it.

CHIEFS:
We have kept vigil around the palace,
As if we knew there would still be a cry.
We have kept vigil around Jokoje,
As if we knew there would still be a cry.

ADEBOYE:
Come friends, let me unveil myself.

CHIEFS:
Keep yourself with yourself.
We have heard and seen enough.
We have heard the death – cry of a queen-mother.
We have heard of the death of a son
Trapped in the fire with which
He was burning down the house of his father.
We have heard of the fall of kings
And the disappearance of traitors.
Keep yourself with yourself,
We have heard and seen enough.

ADEBOYE:
Still, friends, I must unveil myself.
I am the crab in your throat.
The scorpion in your anus.
I am Adeboye.

CHIEFS:
Keep yourself with yourself.
We have heard and seen enough.
(Exit Chiefs.)

ADEBOYE:
My son,
If you still hear me,
Bear my words.
I shall pay, I shall pay.
I shall pay with a bargain.
My tears are bitter,
And I shall swim in their river
To you.
Words are not dead.
They will move me nearer to my end.
Can you hear the ripples of my blood?
They say,
'He that has undone himself,
Let him undo his self.'

(Adeboye pulls out his dagger, stabs himself to death and falls on Adewale. A lullaby is raised by a group of pregnant women in a procession. Costumed in wrappers and head-gears of indigo tie-and-dye. They step wearily, but in a neatly choreographed formation about the stage, observed keenly and sympathetically by the chiefs. Balogun and Mogaji place a wrapper of expensive woven fabric over the corpses, just as the lights fade out completely.)

The End.